TOMORROW'S WOMAN

TOMORROW'S WOMAN

GRETA BELLAMACINA

Andrews McMeel
PUBLISHING®

TOMORROW'S WOMAN

Andrews McMeel Publishing
a division of Andrews McMeel Universal
1130 Walnut Street, Kansas City, Missouri 64106

www.andrewsmcmeel.com

20 21 22 23 24 BVG 10 9 8 7 6 5 4 3 2 1

ISBN: 978-1-5248-5409-6

Library of Congress Control Number: 2019950346

Editor: Lucas Wetzel
Art Director: Tiffany Meairs
Production Editor: Elizabeth A. Garcia
Production Manager: Cliff Koehler

Cover photo by Tom Craig

ATTENTION: SCHOOLS AND BUSINESSES
Andrews McMeel books are available at quantity discounts with bulk purchase for educational, business, or sales promotional use. For information, please e-mail the Andrews McMeel Publishing Special Sales Department: specialsales@amuniversal.com.

Dedicated to Robert Montgomery

Foreword by Robert Montgomery

The Magical New Language of the Moons.

> *You write poetry because you want to perpetuate magic*
> *to find in shoulder moves little shudders and things not*
> *unblessed yet by the binary world.*
> *And because you hate this language as it has become,*
> *and want glimpses of Invisible Magics that the material*
> *world has no use for now.*

(from "Birthday Letter for Me and Brautigan" by
Robert Montgomery)

Poetry isn't a language; it is actually a defense against language, or
more clearly, a defense against ordinary language and the terrible
work that ordinary language does in erasing the tangible magic of
the world. It is tangibly magic and thrilling to be alive on this spin-
ning, blue-skied earth, hurtling away from the oil age into a fragile
and ungraspable future, and in Greta Bellamacina's hands, poetry
uncovers this magic—the hidden magic within the everyday—and
amplifies it and gives it a musical light. The language she has
created is instinctive and new and transformative.

Greta writes in a kind of reinvented English where inanimate objects are filled with life—where scissors have hangovers and the lilies on the table are at once in front of you and marching in heaven.

> *Everything lives unnerved*
> *tiny cups and scissors hungover*
> *lilies in heaven marching in glass on the table*
> *our child arranging the sky,*
> *sleeping between the doorway*
> *blue garments an ocean on the bedroom floor.*
>
> *Your scent a kind of black under heaven*
> *all raging and soft*

("Black Under Heaven")

She has an ability to re-enchant the world that I have rarely seen in a contemporary poet. And a way of writing that collapses bodies and buildings together and stabs them with plants and saves them with light.

> *The pipes are filled with mice and black organ mouths*
> *they keep filling up with feet and hands*
> *they have their own abundance,*
> *their own faithlessness*
> *they are jostled with holly and danger*

("39 Weeks")

In her poetry, we feel our bodies connected back to nature, but it is a nature that encompasses our buildings and our wild cities and our arranged trees. These things, after all—being the things we have made—must somehow be connected to our true nature. She takes our bus stops and our ordinary things and connects them back to stars and eclipses and equinoxes and mystical water.

She has written very vividly about her body, and she is a new voice in a line of poets who write about the female body very vividly, such as Anne Sexton and, of course, Sylvia Plath. Because of this, Greta has been called a feminist poet, and her particular kind of feminism is probably most clearly seen in the poem "Tomorrow's Woman."

But there is also the echo of an older tradition of the Surrealist poets in Bellamacina's work. The influence of André Breton directly is most clearly seen in the poem "Vertical Fires of Land" in this collection, but elsewhere too.

> *The night cars that are already-knocked-at doors*
> *with the eyes of god lamps,*
>
> *the night love of dead trees.*
>
> *The five stoned fat of sunlight*
> *behind the night*
>
> *the night's spangle of solace*
>
> *the park firing of birds*
> *the park's angels*
>
> *the unaskingness of grey*
> *the fear of crumbling trophies*
>
> *an unbraided nettle hanging.*
>
> *The night that is your collarbones*
> *the night that is a wife*

the night's common breath

the night watching over the year
and requiting the vertical fires of land with seasore heads

("Vertical Fires of Land")

As a poet, you should struggle and push against the walls of the language you write in; and Bellamacina does this to new levels, and perhaps more brilliantly than any poet of her generation, creating new phrasings in English, which make at first only musical sense.

How I sleep in the memories of you now,
handful laughter, spidering in tin box letters

your smiles that kill me brighter now,
in the isles of our bones that struggle light,

silvers of blue recording each other's ashes.

Small but eternal wood-adorned kingdoms bringing
libraries now, made away from us in stairways

upwards to bedrooms and windowless strangerlessness.

("First Sleepers")

Strangerlessness isn't really a word, of course, but in the context of this poem, it is a lovely and secret new word for love.

Finally, her poetry is a poetry of light. It seems to give word-form to light in the way that people who are gifted with synesthesia might give colour-form to music.

seven dozing swans
rushing so quickly that we mistake them for paper.

And we know all the things, we know now
that the sun always pulls the light back

and we are always solared by dreams,
sabotaging objects
killing quickly, and making us bored

and the gazing electrical shelters
have a home for us.

There is rain and new surviving youth

("The Jungle")

In this poem, the electrical shelters gaze—strange objects are often personified or given subjecthood in Bellamacina's poems. Objects from the close to the far, from the furniture to the stars, take on our emotions and we take on theirs; everything seems to have liquid self-hood and everything seems to be emotionally awake.

spangling to a teenage dream made of clay
flowering and cracking in the wound of the living.

It moves an ink tree supersonic
bluer always and more real, turning like alchemy
rained up oval alive—
a villa of calligraphy squares.

Horses
a small salvation army of conquest dust—

("The World Is Moved by Love")

And often it's like Bellamacina is translating her poems back into English from either a much more ancient or much newer language.

> *Stranded hurricane*
> *so rare you almost enjoy its fizzing ringrags—*
>
> *sent frenzy reading the water for a chance of wedlock,*
> *offering you the ecstasy of wrapped stone games.*
>
> *Still you think of the daisies passing breath,*
> *rising in moonlight and mending everything,*
>
> *you ache their neck strings,*
> *a swan-lion playing a low symphony agreement.*

("The Weight of a Violin")

When *The Paris Review* wrote to the young California poet Robert Lundquist in 1969, to ask permission to publish one of his poems that their editor had come across and liked, they asked him, "What language has this English version been translated from?" Lundquist had written it in English, but a great poem should always feel slightly awkward in the language you find it in, and a really great poem should feel like it's been translated from an unnameable language.

I first read André Breton, Paul Éluard, and Jacques Dupin in translations from French to English by Paul Auster and Samuel Beckett in *The Random House Book of Twentieth Century French Poetry*. To reach what the Surrealists were saying in French, Beckett and Auster strained against the constraints of English in an incredible and muscular way that brought unconventional usage, new mixtures of noun and verb, and eventually new possibilities of what English could do.

Since then, I have believed passionately that poetry in English, to be new, needs to forget the English language as much as possible, the heavy weight of all its structured precedents, and especially the terrible dulling administrative English we are forced to use every day. Twenty years ago, I began to look for a poet who could do that—when I found Greta, I finally found that poet.

You should write to put the thrill and the magic back into existence and to make it look like some poor translator is struggling to translate your words back from a magical language of the moon.

Robert Montgomery

I.

TOMORROW'S WOMAN   1

II.

PREGNANCY   23

III.

LOVE   43

IV.

LOSS, GRIEF, AND THUNDER   69

TOMORROW'S WOMAN

TOMORROW'S WOMAN

Tomorrow's woman has seen war in heaven
she is the blue of light before time draws

she has loved all the women she has heard
in a throat hood
behind an eye inhaling rain.

Above the stars that cannot be filmed
stars that are not known as paradise
known for their isolation,

biographers of pain
too full of memory.

Tomorrow's woman is the colour of night
tomorrow's woman is your child
tomorrow's woman is shelter

she is sex
the last shock against death,
sex the last peace
sex that forgets black and white.

She is the first to hold a bird in her hands
and learn of foreign love
and not melt at the idea of difference.

Tomorrow's woman is too fat
she bleeds because she knows what it is to feel
a whole generation on her hips
and still be seen as empty
a dog
a fiction

a miracle danger
an ocean of plastic
a soft dangle vine nothing
a war child,

face on a stand
eyes too close together,
mouth like a rental car
feet crossed
the oven is on.

Tomorrow's woman is your father
and his mother, and his mother, and his mother . . .

She is undammable
a renaissance of marching women
as strong as morning
as fearless as water
a school in the wind lighting.

Hands like stolen trees
stuck up in the fog,
a library card to Jerusalem
only human in waves

a courtyard of scarlet fire
closed so far down into itself.

It's hard to imagine what kind of God could believe
the Dead Sea was female,
it's hard to imagine what kind of God could believe
that you could float on your back like this not drowning.

CHURCH
poem to Ginsberg on his birthday

Church the heart, church the knees, church the rosy
cheeks, church the head-kissed lands, church the
numbness, church the blizzard soot dodo, church the
burning sun-patience, church the womb shelter.

Church to becoming better, to becoming overcome, to
letting go, to giving up, to the every single connected day
of sunlight.

Church to suffering on insurance, and then surrendering.

Church the tree blunder, church the broken sleep, church
the suburban queens with nails as long as roads and
crown-chamber mind alarms, recording the sky like a
library record.

Not war, not war, just the road, just the breath, just the mountain.

Church on the cloud of death saddle.

Church for sale,

church of the moving sky, the blackness, and the moving sky,
the people, and the moving sky, and the blackness.

The church sleeping a family of fathers singing
hope-love-me-to-the-ashes.

Church the rooster foot amazement, church the
painkillers, church the holy world antique dispossession,
church the church exits, church the crashing fear gone.
Lorca the church, Patti the church, Robert the church

Lucian the church, Mother the church, "Howl" the church . . .

Howl the directory of the ripped balletic hearts on
paranoid wind pulls.

Stranger the church in absolute moonshine buttonholes.

Church the eggs inside the drifting pavement tree roar.

Church the beautiful, the broken, the steeped, the parade,
the enormity, the wall and the church of eclipsed love,
sublime and terrified and kind and here,

the church of here,
now.

LIVING ROOM MIRROR

"Don't look at yourself like you're a criminal
it's too glamorous," this house is Godless.
Our child hasn't learnt his knees
or the broken dreams of the Internet.

There is only our unprescribed love,
not even a word yet
but for you it's Modernism.

I have taken out my arms, made them into curtains
the same ones you wrote about
tied up with red ribbons before you came and made me
believe like the sun.

Awake in mass light abandon,
blazing like the morning rebirthing
a wonder woman giving out candle tapestry

O'child
the eternal sky,
O'child of morning darkness

retirement seems too cheap now
contact muscles and blind settlements make me late now,
all sacred like the space under our bed—
falling luminescence.

WHOLE WORLD ON YOUR HIPS

End period poverty

You missed school today
you missed the chance to make a wind horse,

cos you carry the whole world on your hips
a home, a heartbeat demonstration, a monument

and you have no one to carry the womb of a rose
no one to carry your whole world in harvest moons

you missed school today
and lay in an imagined era.

And you turned into a woman without the classroom
staring the blank page of womanhood
to a sender of cold war

cos you worry the whole world in your forever,
an embarrassed cloudburst over a field of lost rivers

and you have no one to turn to
no one to let the worry mist into.

You turned into a woman without knowing how to be her
you turned into a woman
who is a hidden library nirvana.

You missed school today
you missed the dance works of wild bird keepers.

You forgot to dream and fell asleep
all your ideas were sacked up to the stars

and the music that drips inside of you still
is the magic of pure new snow.

SEA BIRDS

Expansive blue forevers, a live performance
at the town square of stars.
Mother Earth
slow dancing in green velvet magicians.

The sea birds come to show their support
spiring pendulums, dead and still alive—
small airports of gathered whale processions
and invisible life

living namesake threats,

unpacking the arising starling
a slipped myth,
inside of you.

POMEGRANATE MESSENGER

I take in its double path,
a broadcast of tree hush

Iranian desert roulette
typewriter bird-grey.

I applaud its silent alphabet
crouching curl bolt,

I applaud its sentence
searching woman,

I applaud its frost graves
taught hungry.

Blood lip lamp
a hallucination sender,

mouth full of zigged furniture
a pomegranate messenger

mouth full of dusk shoes
splinter crown-caps,

afterbirthed in drowned ice
versing the purple.

It wants to leak
its half-dressed house,

it wants to leak
its unpublished wars.

It wants to leak
its chest tear tremble

dark water miracle,
headstones.

Clasp shaped, unbibled
all red, all between us

a promised benevolence.

CLEAR WATER

In the garden to which I dream
I see an angel made of stone,
her veins are made from sundials and we call her Asilah.

She is sleeping and her dream is of me
we are both in love, old fate has made us gentle
our legs claim to know a better place to be blown.

We walk and play arrows with acorns
in the downrain of October.
The trees hold out their hands above us

as to make the sky a crown,
and us their reigning destiny
two cathedrals lit up in a forest exposed to the night.

Time to time,
we are as clear as water
casting again for fish
we are as clear to water.

No older than pictures of blowing trees
that travel through children.

REVOLUTION

The revolution has mid-heaven eyes
they have been staring down and blinking up

clusters of women holding hands,
their voices black, apocalyptic violet black

dropping land from their bibles.
They are part of an unremembered walk walking

that moves closer and closer to new ghosts,
new buildings in new rain, new languages

holding stories of abandoned bones
recording the last of the tree echo parts

the last of the exhausted red shadows
the last of suppression.

Seasons, animals, mothers
blowing out low soliloquies of love

they have nothing to do with money.
A whole carpark of lights inside water

a whole heart of blood
resting on a whole heart of blood.

They have seen the naming of and renaming
of flying earth that never leaves

but pulls at you harvesting
through the slipping veil of daffodils

in prayers of freedom replacement wings.
Geranium winter reminders

from one weather to another
growing in your kitchen by the sink

crashing a sky pulse in the drains,
a throat of haloing eyes in the wind.

YEARS

And you find the queen bee dried up
love-edged, pillbox sick

still humming the Angel of the North

a yellow dress, once a gift but now
a lake with no time.

Softly spoken, the stars have all been claimed
grief wheel stadiums

descending in backward hurries

temporary eyes, unbranched
they touch each other with their moods,

clutching at cooler bags of sky held like a coffin.

Unable to keep aflush,
dayless lowlands,

unable to stop loving truly,
emptying gateways

blurred world-delights, unsighted
legs unshaven,

and gasping,
you fall asleep still alive.

SEVEN SISTERS
with Robert Montgomery

You are beside me, winter trees, a comrade to the world, a home,
the TV is playing war, we hope for peaceful sunlight.

The children are dressed in black,
they are throwing petrol bombs at the embassies,
throwing electric flowers into the graveyards of capitalism.

The philosopher is counting the slow candles of the icebergs,
noting how many summers we have left.
She is brilliant in her sunlight hat.
Her chest is a pyramid.

The president has retreated to the golf club, he rules in
half sentences.
Coughing up the 1950s his mind is a puddle where
broken dreams sit on the rooftops of abandoned libraries.

New weddings and empty churches, the minarets talk to
the dawn before the sun lights up the city.
The priests are whirling like dervishes in circles, they
pinball off the walls, singing silence.

Diana and the swan ride an open-topped red London bus,
the trumpets beside them play rave music,
LSD trips to the sound of brass bands.
CCTV diamonds for Oyster cards.

God is bored of us now.

She sides with the animals and the weather and they
watch our digital alien rampage, with cool sad eyes.

BODIES

Renewed skin
never the same trace, fingertip

gentle sketched sunflowers
a weeping sewing machine,

grazing the walls like evening ballads
floating earth balloons.

Your back to me
an uncovered palace wall

your back on me
an ambulance carrying life,

it continues to grow
an invisible history

in the measure of a blues
your own grandmother's address book

a small wonderland
like a house mixed up in embroidery

hands in triangles,
birthing dramatic heights

a trolley of love property
resting rebellion

head-to-wing, in poked ariel fire
an old-world sea bird

skin like war on a stage
a winter field in middle snow dust,

rose-tree midwife of windows
daring you by the glass.

Hair of a horse
over a faded clock,

modern hair like rainfall
hunched blackbird dampness

sun breast isles
burning in its nest.

A new ground level
a coppicing love slouch

refurbishing and refurbishing
the same road.

A continual electrical trail
where love comes to retire

where love comes to suspend
a bewitched symbol

a gentle earth undying
a boat in billowing minds

and on the walk home
the child behind you turns on all the lights

all your ruins move closer to my ruins
a whole country, and we begin.

BLACK UNDER HEAVEN

Everything lives unnerved
tiny cups and scissors hungover
lilies in heaven marching in glass on the table
our child arranging the sky,
sleeping between the doorway
blue garments an ocean on the bedroom floor.

Your scent a kind of black under heaven
all raging and soft,
breaking the tracks of summer
a chapel in the fourth wall
always lit up and nursing.

I have become larger in it
a new kind of warm ash
burning up the edges
and bathing out the reality TV government
I have become more winged.

We barely notice the ceiling falling onto our bed
emptying out the ariel stars
that have tracked our whole lives 'til now
walked with us through hysteria
and trees made into empty news.

We live in one room
the BT Tower our lighthouse,
we have become two mothers
we are unearthed, dosing in the scent
that is an eternal morning.

A HUNDRED YEARS SINCE THE DAY OF PEACE
Imagine Peace Tower, in a London sky, Yoko Ono — 2014

A clap for bronze stolen fire
an older just beginning flinch,

handing out ravens for peace songs

light dome spirits, flying in and out, disguised—
the universe still unknown
mirrored in the ravens and the hunted nobodies

pretending luminous flame creatures
moving around like a series of fizzing digital clocks.

The children are all quiet now,
awaiting a white rainbow message.

And you're at the table above all the saints,
the room at the top of the stairs
diligently writing up a symbolic wasteland,

a remembered escalator of ill heavens
a manhood of memory loss,
a piano of broken botanical jungles
a dream of winter

smoking the marriage of vowel radiance.

I'm already in bed, face in the window
stuck to the wall, no TV yet,
just wishing on new rivers

the BT Tower remains concealed.

IN THE MORNING, PENELOPE

The first together is the morning itself
the marrying wish of dew
the first dance of the grass
renewed like a child's clock

the grass sings to the window—
"come down to the sky fields,
come down and rewatch the eclipse,
come down, Penelope."

The early light unaware of the low hum
that entwines the mood of the air,
strangely worshiping
in high memory cries.

And we remember the ghosts better in the morning
the rising light that is always a grace
on the back of the things you love
scattered through the house like Lego.

The bed remains ancient in its ritual of worship
a personal attack against strangers
made up of all its own Trojan wars
hung in literature, undebated.

It is easy to believe that it is a privilege to grow old
in the morning and that age is young
and all that is above will remain immortal
regardless of loneliness.

PREGNANCY

LIFE

I imagine there is a wind
that is blowing away,

but always arriving at full new birthdays

not dead but flying

pouring and pouring transparent stars
through the great surrendering ark skies,

regressing in ancient light that is heavy
because it lugs the dilemma of ancient light,

blowing the accidentalness
of things that hang

and the perpetualness of just hanging on.

I watch the temperature
a low battery light cure—

wave and go cooler
to the thought of emptying the dishwater

a gentle digression, opening away
and letting it all just go, to a hallelujah'd turning.

It keeps blowing
and occasionally stopping

to give way to a family
floating bags of water.

I see a face, it is a face I love,

it pours a kind of counter-light
to the rest of the strange past

and invisible future,
my own mother, the sea,

the sea
carrying anarchic oceans on her back.

LIFE AUTOMATIC

Nothing can break this travelling silence
unsettled hypnosis,

unable to swing the double doors
and sit beside its own daytime latency.

It is the denial of life automatic
it has no space

the raking of the sky has no taste for it,

it sort of pleases you anyway,
like a young horse willing the garland candle-flowers.

Suspended waltz
where breathing is a lifted scalpel,

the ground auditions heights
unattached rooftops
unattached, like a lover's hair clipping.

It has nowhere to go and still it has been 14 days
and again it has been normalised by daytime faces

continually withdrawing all action
like blank battleship wood
left on a beach sunken and reduced to notions of left
tidal waves

thoughtless memories
long-ago sweethearts.

17 WEEKS

There hasn't been much to break
just this ache
blood-fire-Jesus towards me,

picked up, ageless worm
rolling in the serenity of a lake
to a messenger of quiet answers, deeper inside

bluer and more critical than the sky

throbbing quicker than the erotica of fuchsia,
shutdown twice'd wool

opinions pretend black suns.

I body every gap masculine edge
I body every lit light
I body every bit of rent
I body every miserable strand hoop

that catches round the future,
every disappearing cry that
hands out order.

I body the poem of my body
where I can live like a gypsy at sea
conducting the distant ships.

PALE GOLD

The flowers grew much quicker than everyone expected,
they pulled their faces to the world
shivering thoughts of love and
oxygen—
pale gold refugee towers

made like mythology
tiny prisms of anniversary encores,
dancing to the renewal of land-dew peace
gentle reminders of hope and
wreckage undone.

20 WEEKS IN WATER

I have felt you drinking back the 20 weeks
like it was a steep haunting
like it was too far for you,

some kind of unnamed holiday
neither a question of bearable sleep
nor locked up water

keeping you closer to me without control.
A tossed violet lineage
washed in synchronised ivy

weeping to the erotica of purple
weeping to the same lake, serenity
which is the size of a football

vanishing back a flat eternity,
non-academic nor sophisticated in this water
in this heatwave of unfinished whiteness

a guest of single answers
with familiar nerves,
drowning out the ungathered, reported twilight

a guest of a woman
smuggling fire,

dressed like broken atmosphere,
puffing a Bunsen burner bouquet.

A guest of a woman
feeling a hundred bathing doves inside of her kickback
devouring everything that sinks.

20–WEEK SCAN

Halfway to clear blue,
where the end is vivid yellow, where all your sensations stay
longer than this immeasurable space of waiting.

Tiny hospital screens and shut away measurements,
halfwayed despair rivers, new weddings
out of date.

Longer than the arms that carry them
already self-bathed,
cultivated marble

screaming, heaven's heartbreak is for free.

Already unneeded,
a connection to all women
fallen and risen

heartbreak to their utopian celebrities
their second homes,
stories of fruit gifts

leftover rubbish on a fallen river.

You think about how close you feel
to everything that leaves you—
everyone you once knew, eventually goes deeper inside.

The Internet is full of eagles, they cry out from all the
isolated fullness, pushing like bread

they remind you of a storybook.

A whole world science fiction,
to outlive you.

Images made out of unrolled eyes
and due dates, butterflying hands,
self-paragraphed

halfway from now, calling,
"white chords of extra vows,
white chords of extra vows."

THE BETTER GERANIUM

I like to pretend
I don't care as I pour you a lake
from my kitchen sink.

I pour you my tears
wide-wept dunes, to the
geranium hero liver.

I reorder my ways,
cos my friends told me
it was the right way.

I hope you will stay better,
I say it, but I don't know it.

You will go, because I will go,
in innocence when innocence is coming apart.

A less to lessen us both
my daytime idol, as it appears,
bacteria I grew.

STOCKHOLM SYNDROME

There is a lake inside of me now
a Catherine wheeled eyehole,
it has devoted itself to my whole body
naturalised by the sense of smiles.

It has thrown away the traffic on Liverpool Street
and muted the dangers of collapsing eggshells,
unmistakably breaking

travelled spat watering tides.

It does not stop growing,
I do not stop pretending to notice.
It is like a kind of backstage womb
to a dreamless love,

dealing in water
webbing a North Star secret,
brushing out a wheel of needlework.

Reduced to love

protecting a hush, it tells you the name of the biggest star,
you think of it unseen tying like a bow,

and how stranger you'd never thought to imagine, on this bed of
waxed awakenings

a new weeping benevolence, unstoppable, uncommon,
giving back the earth this vast length of wing time,
like the throat of an eagle.

You are your own midwife of birthdays,

I've seen you contemplate your own solitude,
the handful ruins quiet restlessness.

Viagra water flickering through morning tea
tribes of water burning the air,
and white heat that is a renamed cover version of water.

Where I am young girl made from stolen deep purple red,
made at the same time as the leaves
under no threat, linking to the earth like an undisturbed
birdsong.

WAITING ROOM HANDS

There is a poster in the waiting room,
it says, *"bond with your baby, bond with your man"*

both hands smother a single breast,
like all nature is a Freudian crippling—

unowned shadows connect to the same thick shoe straps
snipping out the hugs of eavesdropping children

to less important memories of laughter that call you "mama,"
posthumous, nurse unpronounceable.

Amusing the uncontrollable sunlight that is florescent
and parched by the inherited morning sun.

Shading out the manying metaphors for hands,

the trampled will of hands,
the hands themselves that hold you until you hold them back,

and how their surprisingly slender mightiness is
mistaken for protection.

INSTA
with Robert Montgomery

Broad blue, armoured like this
everything is all stacked up
lined and taken home
like-shunted
from this to this
cavern of popularity

most popular posts of the day
a reduction of everything
"based on people you follow"
Followers: 28k
recurring reasons for meaningless suicide

and we measure
light now like this
so sorrowing the way we always wished
percentage by passage the dug-out October
tambourine flowers all made,
young-made like this.

NEW GLASS

We hold up the new gods of our post-electric reality.

Echo our dreams into empty rooms,
shelter the strange television flowers that try to seduce
us away from the memory of weather.

But outside there is new rain. Twenty-five sets of hands
to make you feel at home.

When you close your eyes, you hear the sound of wind
trapped behind the police station like a sacrifice.

You think back to all the homes you once sold yourself,
the eyes behind the hotel windows, facing out on a cold
Euston station.

How you live further than trying to sleep now.

The kingdom is in recess,

we have built love a blanket and put sticks in it like a tent,

we have let the land own it and protect the people who find it.

We tell their stories, choir the threads of it, make friends
with the birds who fly in and out of the Wi-Fi signals.

We sing new wonder at our collective hope, and make new glass
from it.

39 WEEKS

The pipes are filled with mice and black organ mouths
they keep filling up with feet and hands,
they have their own abundance
their own faithlessness

they are jostled with holly and danger
never more than the past and less than the space of a heart.
You mistake them for midnight cleaners
and drunk bus stops

swept away sterilised from birth.
Candelabras melting whiter than Christmas
vibrating hot water iron ovaries
and further driftwood shadows,

siren angel replacements.

But every time we sleep all darkness gives up
and becomes a secret manifesto
stating the erosion of things
and consolation of things combined.

I cannot tell what is yours or mine or his anymore
it does not indebt me like I think it should,
it does not present
ail blue, ail blue, anymore.

UMBILICAL ARRIVAL

I have found myself in a rushed unfasten
a nervous curse of calm,
unarmed and burning a non-religion

my funeral finally ending,
beating daytime through bought carpet
and extra doors to keep the night from gazing

a heart-drought uncoil,
a well working factory villain
pulling on string

a hotel balancing on rain,
a family of shoes lined up on the tip of a shriek
and the sky turning in the recycling.

A black tickle unable to keep its shape,
like a young-eyed wolf-dandelion
in the supermarket, unhooking the onions

cleaning the days of the week
like the cemetery at the end of our road
dressed up in poetry and the seasons,

a rare pull-in of mercy
a tide waiting to fill the shore.

THE LAST 60 SECONDS OF MORNING

Thunder first, locked up in babble
rain-eyed gods on their backs

you stayed in the forefront
black ribbon angel, headless,

four standing roses and a background of wind-split
you died in America for the last time

Jason Molina holding all the horses
behind the last slip-dawn rain

I cannot live in a place that doesn't save its people in time
I cannot live in a place that doesn't live out its own odyssey

so the myths are paralyzed
the myths are luminous riddles

the horses are all full
the saints are blood cannons

love is a vacuum mist
a showed weekend of dreams on repeat

a distant screen to both worlds
a second think to the running light

10 seconds where morning is at one with daytime
clasping in the change of lightness

lugging the stones of womanliness
peaking and popping when everything breaks

10 seconds where morning is at one with daytime
a spin of patter, a direction that needs no explanation

downwards to the earth
a curtain of chances,

a slide of swan dance
swaying in animal timing

the last joy to morning is the memory
the animals are laughing

grasping forward they escape
light continues to slide out

the gods are asleep now and far away
a preview of reflections borders the world

night is lowered to day and the actors arrive
worrying their costumes.

LOVE

THE WORLD IS MOVED BY LOVE

The world is moved by love
it is set free by it
a peace body saviour
a radio siren promise

spangling to a teenage dream made of clay
flowering and cracking in the wound of the living.

It moves an ink tree supersonic
bluer always and more real, turning like alchemy
rained up oval alive—
a villa of calligraphy squares.

Horses
a small salvation army of conquest dust—

a surrendered mystical chest
watching arms in hands
interlocking hearts like netted curtains.

The marketplace in tomorrow's new dawn,
travelling bells found inside Lazarus

a butterfly in abandoned heaven.

We exist in the waterside a clasp of mercury mother
fist-full and ageless.

It feeds you just as it leaves you
it makes you believe just as it shows you
the writing of the cold wind
on the gates of heaven.

WHEN THE MORNING COMES

When the morning comes
your love renews like an imagined river,
always cradling in eternal light.

When the morning comes
your love remains dream-sighted,
out of time like a dazzling stone
from the ocean.

When the morning comes
your love is like hope,
promising life like sudden sun.

When the morning comes
your love moves like a red forest,
hem locking revolutions.

When the morning comes
your love brings the promise
of morning behind the night,
wide and somewhere close.

When the morning comes
your love covers like a beach,
a whole coast of classical findings.

When the morning comes
your love is unvanquished,
asking where to go next.

When the morning comes
your love is a phantom future,
astonishing and gazing in its break.

LONDON FIELDS

with Robert Montgomery

Travel under me
high salutes of morning sadness
sliding the copper

I have nothing to give you but upside-down geraniums
no mansions

caught up in
orange sun blighting

giving the overed,
no blinding orange sun.
I've only worked this day.

Garage-hidden gifts and Vicks VapoRub,
deep diamonds and stolen trainers,
the summer rubs up, Hackney is on fire again,
CCTV cameras turn on automatically
all over our city,
to record the poverty with which I love you.

THOUSAND TEARS OF HOPE

My love whose heart
is a thousand tears of hope
haloing from all the forgotten
gardens of sleep,

ending skyloss, five years
making up the breeze
sliding,

wings twice made from stone
a half-diagonal Notre Dame,
filled with impossible
monuments

lighting carriages on frankincense,
and ancient bonfires signaling
new life.

THE FIRST BURNT STAR

The first burnt star,
in the silence of water

a gold thunder
dazzling a lion benediction moon

The stars, the stars, the stars,
they land in your dreams,
stone white teeth

five points like a sundial
beckoning to the trees, turning in the wind's mouth

They land on bits of wheat
like secret messages from the sun,
large against the iron bells.

Before there was anything
there were the stars touching time with hope,

before there was anything
love was still blind in the darkness,

all of wonder above you,
where you put it, up high.

The stars, the stars,
beside you, somewhere in the future
falling in grave-rain

Freedom blows like a feather,
sweeping out an eternal call
like a bird who cannot explain why peace is in its wings

You are reminded again of the sky
a flower of dust, dancing like a snow globe
emptying out its possessions for you

Before there was anything,
everything was hailing,
all our hearts were comets up in the sky
and everything was hailing.

WHEN YOU WAKE

When you wake the cities you love
are somewhere behind you,

all of Europe is a flooded dream of collective beauty
the weather is drawing squares

a jewellery box of godless dreams
encircling light brings Babylon with it

it holds the secret history of pain
it holds the yellowing embrace of strangers

suitcases filled with rivers to a third paradise
out-guessed with laced silver.

Michelangelo disappears into a cloud
holding *"Love feeds the flame of age."*

I think of my own children
and how they exist in images of colour

how their eyes carry bells ringing
yew tree wishes.

Outside the mountains hang a string of glass stars
chorus signs of erased words,

the oceans are filled with reason
they reflect us in their wake

the oceans have all been given death letters
no one is surprised in time

all conclusions are left unopened
their mouths remain shut.

Before bed you discover you are only at Paris
the slowness is flowering

the forests lean into tracks
they whisper broken sounds of freedom

the morning is somewhere else
at night the flowers read the day in fallen things

it frees you all the same
that no country can escape the need to move closer.

PERISHING TAME

We haven't seen the morning together for a while
that vague paralyzing quiet
stripped of shock,

I know you have relocated
gallowed up, still poor,
we were children then
razored reckless and abducted in our bedrooms.

All my paranoia and bones stuck into you
and all yours grew into my imagination
a female saint,
a male Madame Bovary alley cat,

gales of perishing tame.

We have died next to each other
and lived in the faces of songs
stealing the birds
wrapped in the bags of wildflowers

I have poured everything out.

You have been my television
a waistcoat anthology on Charlotte Street
coffee for January.

The pain of being asked to
when I thought I was just sewn up,
and you know it too,

like all of the lost things that end up further away
buried cutlery in the Heath's forgotten parrots.

Homeless, but we sleep now away from the floors

and the day we buried your mother
I remember you said, I can't imagine
I can't think of the weight
all those porcelain palls
and grey glass tans.

They have not been you yet,
but have contained your gold old younger pains
dreamed of a different broken second midnight,

drainted, the image of your parents in a kaleidoscope
all standing proud and doped
all provocatively snow
unfair grey, dangerous and boring on the market day

something about the clouds
and the modern dead ideas
Mary and June bathwater.

STARLIGHT

In the night your eyes
watch mine like searchlights in the snow
there is a thread from my heart
direct to yours and it is held tight in the starlight,
always holding out the cold.

COLLAPSE OF THE WORLD

When hell spat you back
enclosed from the collapse of the world
from the panic of the dispatches
saved from the disintegration
faces towards the blank sky
tracing the memory of the birds.

POST–VALENTINES POEM

Your arms are sunset sonnets
made of pavement oak
filling the rain passing,

altering the winds to the country tide
eight hundred ways, manned by the atlas of longer worlds.
Your love it is skywards for

the hold of gentle eyes
that surround the river's skin
only to break deathstones for time in the sky.

Back to your house built to wood
back in the almost horizon sun,
your love is the eve of.

Gazing down every street
unmorninged heights
of the many ways you can marry in "high windows,"

read in the windfelt light birds
of distanced swung skies
that are left to you, which are setting.

DARTMOOR WEDDING SONG

Dartmoor came with a low fog—
the ancient gods all sleeping between the
sky cloud torches,

the same as the bed we woke up in
anti-clockwise flagstones
hung heroes, chattering rain songs.

Shaking the locking organed funfairs

the daytime observes its place to the sun,
bewitched by the size of the hills.

There is a line of trees,
broken star pillars
silently on the roadside still-stung

free angeled ebony bird tombs.

Born again to moors
forking the heartlands

washing in the mystery of Sunday
and the ferrying images of you pushing the pram
up the hill towards me,

barely a shape
grappling with this idea of distance
and the abandonment of paradise hurt.

FIRST SLEEPERS

How I sleep in the memories of you now,
handful laughter, spidering in tin box letters

your smiles that kill me brighter now,
in the isles of our bones that struggle light

silvers of blue recording each other's ashes.

Small but eternal wood-adorned kingdoms bringing
libraries now, made away from us in stairways

upwards to bedrooms and windowless strangerlessness.

Uncollected, still, you made me sleep like a queen
on the manyed floor
over sheets that don't cheat minds but marble
staring teary courtroom dramas,

storming through the oceans that pour the insides.
First sleepers,
in a house of local men and rooms that sleep
with fingers which pray each other for safety.

Is this really the end?

Bad dreamers we must have been,
with your lakefire eyes,
with my maze snake thread
escaping every time, burning through the taps.

There are so many ways to see the wisteria
in the Medina, from the French horizons of before Fez.

Tanning the shadow of the high-up bodies
in your mouth, which is the wellspring
still cleaning me anyway
in thunder and loss.

DEATH

Love, the last shock against death
Love, the last symbol of peace.

THE DREAMERS

They said we won't be able to
survive on a pink cloud
that we should take each day as it comes
watch the sand angels fall to death
whilst we were sleeping in the low noise.

They said we should be famous
live blackened gold,
lovesick, the stars on your pillow

let the daydreamers sink in the arrears,
unearthing.

Break away from the ancient light
on your council flat,
the sky between the piles of clothes
and the painted forest cords—

pay yourself a whole working heart,
boxing the day like this.

The last symbol of romance
your mattress made of airtime
your sleep that is a longer heaven.

SILENT LANGUAGES

My love whose heart
is a house of broken maps
and silent languages that stay through the weather report
and strangers at the door.

A filled galley rowing towards
crashing waves.

DRAWN NECKS

My love whose arms are the drawn necks
of midsummer roses and raincloud predictions,
whose arms are the foreign
dictionaries of lovers

who own nothing but ideas of new
civilizations we will never reach.

PHOSPHORESCENT

Your love is a kingdom of escape.
Start with nothing,
rebuild everything sacred.

ABOVE WATER

Faraway I put the memory of you above water,
and send it out as a paper boat.

THE PERSEID METEOR SHOWER

The Perseid meteor shower was a 100,000-year-old cry
of shooting tears, 600 an hour rolling down in one direction.

They fell into the sea, they fell into the peeled trees,
they fell like gentle raindrops copying tears that cry,
found near earth, rare dead raindrops, moving in sinister
muse-like eyes.

They fell into shadow pictures, they fell into the cold traps,
they fell truths apart from long ago that just grew bluer
weeping the sounds of number eights.

They fell into the landscapes of a man
they fell into the landscapes of a criminal

they all glowed lamplight ballads that surpassed the
debris only to show eight gold lines like ageless vines.

They looked sad, like they had come to find you there in
serenading fireworks.

But could only see the next decade,
and how it would be the same as the night of similar strangers.

Lovers were advised to take blankets
to keep sight, look up and then down
bullets elegantly fading like blowing light.

A couplet to do,
a good way above
tiny flames leaving the air like sentinel wedding cakes,
mistaken rocks like evening seeds,

sword scriptures, which were once the fingers of
waterfall brains but now sand that is old
resting on sand that is new,
and sand that is pale and unshaken.

They looked like love,
they looked like us.

LOSS, GRIEF, AND THUNDER

AFTERLIGHT

We found out that Leonard Cohen died this morning
and the world was reminded of poetry
the pale domes of white light
all singing faraway from where we sleep,

flame-shadowing gods everywhere
down the Tottenham Court Road
trapped up in treelight
lost in the light of the kitchen

you hold onto me and say
where do they go
the torpedoing shadows that fill the world,
where the moon tries to draw closer and touch love
but doesn't quite make it through the fog.

And how death could be the only way to reunite
and return to music
and find a different kind of peace,
again how the angels must have known already
without the intent of prayers.

The long long afterlight
stored up in the day,
shattering the harshness of the blank world.

But still it rains at home

and like you, poetry still haunts everyone
like the way we brought our baby home from the hospital
all blue and breathed up
covered in traffic
a swaying heaven ship.

The new air of our flat is gentle,
a cradle of ships all resting
making the afterlight command
a nameless world, all static and in us

we all forgot to be homesick
unhurt by the thought of paradise,
rowing forward to a world full of beaconing wishes
like a winter of broken-up keys.

Forward to a graceful whisperer
making us mad again
and holy again like the commonness of a table face,
nursing like a bed next to a chair.

Forward again to the unseen notion of shores
playing hell violins
chaining loss

but really moving us closer to our own need for love.

Love that is unwarred for

safer in the sky
closer to the birds
who hold your dreams like lullabies
filled with a downslope of pressed hands.

I have woken in a window
and existed from both sides now,
the morning is a train
the afterlife is a horse

travelling back to you—
arms wide open
growing in the cupboard,
a hyacinth stretching
out into the first daylight.

MISSING EUROPE

I made up our bed, a clean wedding
thought I would find you in it.
Thought we had the same eroding mouths
when you swallowed my language
I didn't care because the secrets of my past
were yours too and I counted how many women I could be.

I felt lighter than all the metal flags between us
the ones that made up our alibi stars,
arrows breaking up miles and the value of chicken.
And below we were their immigrant lovers
marching paradise futures, filling up the diary you carry
around like a small echo healer.

And we laughed at the big brother forecast,
until we could no longer understand why
we were both missing.

VERTICAL FIRES OF LAND

The unbearable night
the night building that washes water

the night wind that sounds like trapped radiator spirits

the night red light mill
the night full of ship tears

the mystery that calls you old-fashioned
the night meadow of drafts

the water you would plant under the ground
to save a generation.

The night walls that shudder flowers
the night woman who is bare,

the equal distances from arms and closed eyes
and gardens that make a city wide.

The great face of street kingdoms

the letting of strangers with metal-coloured necks
and the sexes of swans.

The night cars that are already-knocked-at doors
with the eyes of god lamps,

the night love of dead trees.

The five stoned fat of sunlight
behind the night

the night's spangle of solace

the park firing of birds
the park's angels

the unaskingness of grey
the fear of crumbling trophies

an unbraided nettle hanging.

The night that is your collarbones
the night that is a wife

the night's common breath

the night watching over the year
and requiting the vertical fires of land with seasore heads

the unforgiving night.

The polite notion of restarting
and the barking of roses

the night skin of summer,

the eight ways you became brother and sister
for the sake of rainwater

freely whiter than burnt wood.

UNOCCUPIED

We lie sideways like surviving water in a lost pool
and make the tracks of black seeds
blending into the renaissance of the sea,
turning England somewhere.

We have packed up our lives several times now
the rehearsal of the rain has poured over our hearts,
pinwheeling a dressmaker hellion.

We have thrown out all the ashed up voices

let the flowers open like maps,
families of brick wall primroses
clutching and flaunting closer.

We have embraced all the parts of just time
fading and fading,
like the way the word itself seems to melt in your mouth flake-sided.

We have become old dreams
lying on hourglass traps
boarded up like embarrassed commitments.

We criticise all of the unpoetry
all the pointless nights that haven't been written down—
asking no questions of the world

but still we walk home alone.

We wonder why this trick has become available
several love lives later,
along the Southbank like a row of rained-on books.

We assure ourselves 7:59, O'children
lifting up our children,
embarrassed angels.

We declare ourselves
two prisoners, detached doors
terrible twos.

We trample the white conceal

a turn-of-the-century tree
a portfolio of weeping inspections.

We have said goodbye, like the first time
closing down our immigrant selves,
dozing on cinema.

All comforting along Pigeon Square
we wound the bird-feather's cosmology,
and again the bottomless grey of pigeons.

We have become neighbours,
with all the rightness of snow
all the brightness of hot meals.

We have held every shanty star
and reinvented ourselves in
unoccupied land

washing like an index.

THE JUNGLE

Every day the sunlight pours over The Jungle
and I can't help think,
what if we fell in love, again.

If we were to meet out of this time
seven dozing swans
rushing so quickly that we mistake them for paper.

And we know all the things, we know now
that the sun always pulls the light back

and we are always solared by our dreams,
sabotaging objects
killing quickly, and making us bored

and the gazing electrical shelters
have a home for us.

There is rain and new surviving youth
and like mindless babies
we share everything that wakes up.

There is guilt and spit and commercial love
drowning space and cold currents,

like the time I wrote that we were unblessed
but we only take Suzanne on a boat
and she becomes the only one to walk on the water

and her blindness is lost
and the leaning lovers hold out their hands
and all of the captured strangeness is vanished

there is a twin light
it is bewitched and not yours anymore

and we don't know if the light is just fainting
if the heads of the new trees are nothinged
by The Jungle if you don't come too.

And we just shake
and we just quake

the view of the drains and the birds
are grown to be mad

jutting Paris, jutting Calais
jutting Syria, jutting law and established dreaming aha!

Five stepping oranges
and faintlight holes and nobody who helps

and we just shake our brains
yearn our numbers
empty it all out
print adriftness.

And we are precious of our hurt
our mouths out wet
think warrant wetness
tinderboxed in fire that just kindles.

MAY TREES

Everything comes back to this
you sleeping beside me
a double victory underworld

low and distorted
a heart of public property stars.

I could fall deeper and still the sky
dangles its embrace over the May trees

a carpenter of still life
upwards into the earth's blackening

tossing out the air
for the light to heaven its peace

broken air like empty weapons
from an unwritten poem.

Stonehenge hung up in the bedroom
a multicoloured kiss
a knot marching distance

a wedding.

THE WEIGHT OF A VIOLIN

Stranded hurricane
so rare you almost enjoy its fizzing ringrags—

sent frenzy reading the water for a chance of wedlock,
offering you the ecstasy of wrapped stone games.

Still you think of the daisies passing breath,
rising in moonlight and mending everything,

you ache their neck strings,
a swan-lion playing a low symphony agreement.

Like the sun giving you everything
a heavy flash of hope with only a billion years
to understand its divided oranged dawn.

Below we swing in and out of belief
unpacking the centre

wooden lungs,
played through interludes of dark fascinations,
wrists weeping the hard awake

it changes you,
it remains unchanged

feeding you seeds like a castaway, a flowered asylum—
unashamed by its own tragedies.

It leads you back to the sky
to a cribbed wind of sea

a sideways persuasion—

the weight of a violin
leaving out nothing,

but the notes of the blue trees
against the clouds unrest.

WHALE NATION IN A PLASTIC BAG

The ocean is filled with broken dreams now
it shrinks a tomb of hands all reaching out for the sky

stone dictionaries in plastic bags,
agonize stone wings in ink gulls.

Whale Nation in a plastic bag
breaking like a heart,
blankets of exhausted geography.

The birds are filled with plastic too,
emblazoning emotions in empty bottles
that never sink, that never hold you
imagine you in mercy.

To feel it like this, to decamp the mirth as it lays
and then to feel it at that moment of hurl,
wheelchairing gravity

the great abandonment of light
a quarter vale needing to find something to shelter with

and to spotlight in,
out of the darkness and to heaven in
a nightfall within the living.

Hymned on the burnside

and you have to praise it anyway
cos it breaks you in two

unending the seven seas—a heavy named waterstar
all in a backwards birth.

AFTERWARDS
for my dear Daisy Boyd

Post-hearted and regretted
we find you already fallen

autumn always kills me
the trees let go silvering fierce

the show is on the ground
the sky annihilating a merry-go-round

London is no longer famous
the children are buzzing fingertips,

a paper bag of tears named Diana
ceremonial stone walls.

A cigarette end gasping a golden rope
an arrow of the past

I don't know how many times we've moved house
to find space for dreaming.

All of our old letters remain the downpour
unable to disturb the living

Ophelia is in the wind somewhere on the coast
leaving the sand to announce its suffering.

The summer before comes back to haunt us
abandoned crows

Bunhill Fields undated
the remains of lovers

prepared like a porcelain dinner,
always promising and staggering.

INDIAN YMCA

Precipice of lamplight
dark circles where pink flowers sleep,
thumping between tube stations
always the promise of orange sun.

There is no allotment for this blue rehearsal

we have replaced our faces like old caretakers,
overwinged by the thought of secret exits

bluer than the untangle of a ballroom.

All that is free kills you now

even the light doesn't save you in time,
it stays with you in the hospital

the edge of mannerless silence.

All around London annotates the dead parties,
the insides of houses
a greyhound runner

scarfed with electric carpet shocks.

This year the Indian YMCA has Christmas decorations
all ropy, a silvering choker
backed on the corner of Fitzroy Square

floating foreign light, like it too has forgotten itself
still it stays open.

EAST WINDOW
East Window at St. Martin-in-the-Fields

Three years and we have been trading
hands for more understanding

living between the feathers of flying birds
batting out war for a rewritten love.

East window always awake
set at the altar of Trafalgar Square

appendix hailing red
we are the children writing it,

only here for a day
two hearts in a ruin.

Nothing ever vanishes
it just stands in the clouds

still we walk closer
a crucifix and a halo

daylight in the living
Adonis in your mind leftover,

midmorning escapes
flickering Victorian gown circuits,

everything is opened out
the river is as full as a womb.

Jagged light lies
on its side pointing to the stars

calling back to the wanderers,
they do not breathe stop.

The immortal waltz
revolving in grid stamps

no end to the pieces
just the start deeper again

the cliff in the sky
the seagulls sleeping on God

peace giving height
stones in the skull.

DAWN BREAKING

The gods met up to decide your fate first
they made their decision through the "rosy-fingered dawn"

the wind was young and they sat on the broken spells of rain.

A dozen owners of the stars
throw down their signals,
an inter-wind of eagles to see if you'd notice.

A clapped window seat
made like a shaking train far in your childhood—

for you to roam the cold streets
for you to imagine the end of the sky
and the school you will one day leave.

To see if you would notice me
walking coatless by the ghost of our thunder.

The night continues to note down the morning dawn

it breaks slowly, gentle like a smile
ragged with hand-peddles from a mountain seascape.

The light is egoless at this hour
it is in a state of meditation

it rows pulling Eden back,
in a sapphire box of pills.

It is a woman and a man
it is the quest of prayer-wheels

giving the light the latency of light.

You're fast asleep beside me rafting with the tides
you have your own birds, hallowing you unbonded,

but the birds inside of me have not stopped
flapping their towering wings in twos,
another Mediterranean inside a drum.

Athena stayed behind like a statue in darkness
holding the torchlight towards Troy

remembering the honour of peace
remembering the hour of waking
remembering the bureaucracy of tears.

The heavens remain unimpressed
their one job—biographers of the light

a freezer tray to the sky
where all golden light comes to die
and to live in between the voices of a set of pearls
rewriting a postcard to ash.

And you're awake now and everything is settled and you say,
"I can feel it, it's alive."

A MESSAGE OF THANKS

To Robert Montgomery, who has been my lighthouse. An endless trail of hope and support. The first person to buy me a cooker after years without one. The first person to look out at the BT Tower with the same dream. My octane angel of the sky, beating eternal Window Hymns.

To my boys, Lorca and Lucian Valentine, who have the hearts of wild horses running in rain. Thank you both for giving me a home when I thought I was always going to be homeless.

To my mother, Cynthia, for always being strong and fearless. Holding us together and making us brighter. For giving us all life. For your rebel spirit and heart.

To my father, Benny, for giving me the confidence to keep writing, to keep dreaming, to keep going. For keeping me in the sunlight and giving me nature.

To Daniel Dowek, for being there for me, selflessly and truly like a guardian angel. For piecing my words together.

To Louis, Camilla, Cosima, and Sylvie, for beating the same stars.

To Lucas Wetzel, for giving my poems a life and letting them live in the world.

To Clare Conville, for believing it could all happen.

Additional thanks to the hero-dreamers: Brit Parks, Heathcote Williams, Natalie Hand, Heathcote Ruthven, George Khayat, Ana Seferovic, Robert Lundquist, Susan Bradley-Smith, Oscar Jahme-Dunbar, Michael Horowitz, Julie Goldsmith, Niall McDevitt, Jaclyn Bethany, Sylvia Whitman, Fabio Paleari, Janette Montgomery, and Juan José Vélez Otero.

Special thank-you to Tom Craig for the cover picture.

ABOUT THE AUTHOR

Greta Bellamacina studied English at King's College London. Her first self-published collection, *Kaleidoscope*, saw her short-listed for Young Poet Laureate of London in 2014. In 2015, she edited *On Love: A Collection of Contemporary British Love Poetry*, a survey of British love poetry from Ted Hughes until now.

She has since published two books with the small London poetry press New River Press—the poetry collection *Perishing Tame* in 2016 and *Collected Poems 2015-2017*. *Collected Poems 2015-2017* has been translated into a Spanish-language edition by Valparaíso Ediciones. In 2018, she was commissioned by the National Poetry Library to write a group of poems for its Odyssey series.

Greta has been the writer-in-residence at Chateau Marmont in Los Angeles. *Interview* magazine says she "is garnering critical acclaim for her way with words and her ability to translate the classic poetic form into the contemporary creative landscape."

Her work has been featured in the *Guardian*, *The Times*, *Dazed*, *i-D* magazine, *Interview* magazine, *Vogue*, and the *London Magazine*. She has performed her poetry on CNN, *BBC World News*, *BBC Radio 4*, *BBC London*, *BBC Radio 2 with Jonathan Ross*, *BBC Radio 3* on *The Verb* poetry show, and live at The Poetry Café in London and Shakespeare and Company in Paris.

Greta is also an actor and filmmaker. In 2016, she made the activist documentary *The Safe House: A Decline of Ideas*—a love letter to public libraries and an appeal against their closure. And in 2019, she wrote and directed the feature film *Hurt by Paradise*, which was nominated for the Michael Powell Award for Best British Feature Film at the Edinburgh International Film Festival, and Best UK Feature Film at Raindance. It will have a cinema release in 2020.

Tomorrow's Woman is her first poetry collection to be published internationally.

Enjoy *Tomorrow's Woman* as an audiobook narrated by the author, wherever audiobooks are sold.